WOMEN IN THE WORKPLACE: A MAN'S PERSPECTIVE

Lloyd S. Lewan

Written with
Ronald G. Billingsley, Ph.D.

RP

Remington Press: Denver, Colorado

Book design by Leslie Gabriel
Photography by Kimball Hall

For Information
  Remington Press
  P.O. Box 24187
  Denver, Colorado 80224-0187

ISBN 0-9620360-0-5
Library of Congress Catalog Card Number: 88-90731

Printed by
  Johnson Publishing Company
  1880 S. 57th Court
  Boulder, Colorado 80301

"Dr. Lewan's presentation is thought-provoking and refreshingly candid. It is essential reading for those who want to see men and women working together as equals."

Patti Digh-Howard
American Association of
State Colleges and Universities

"The most innovative presentation addressing gender issues I have ever heard."

Mrs. Jerry D. Sheely, President
Colorado National Bank-Boulevard

"At last a man writes the truth about men's attitudes toward women at work. I wish this had been published forty years ago. I agree wholeheartedly."

Roger L. Williams
Retired Executive
Continental Trailways Bus System

"This is an excellent concept. The only long term strategy for institutional success should include the unfettered contributions of men and women."

Lua R. Blankenship Jr., President
Children's Hospital, Denver

"This is must reading for men and women who want to work successfully together. I have learned much that I am now applying in my own business."

Elizabeth Abbott
For Men Only, Inc.
Interior Designs

"Finally, here is a man who has the courage to tell it as it is. This is a superb book."

Kathy Cannataro
Teacher, Aurora Public Schools

"A most timely and exceptionally revealing diagnosis of the hurdles American women face today. A natural speaker, Lloyd captures the essence of today's work environment with his uncanny realism."

Susan Blake
Hanover Security Reports, Inc.

This book is dedicated with love to

———————◆———————

Kimberly Ann Lewan

Vida Jocelyn Billingsley

Acknowledgments

First and foremost, we want to thank our families for their indulgence and patience during this long process of reducing our ideas to paper.

We offer a special note of thanks to the men and women who read the early copies of this work and provided much insight and help: Elizabeth Abbott, Henry Beer, Robin Royce Blake, Susan Blake, Vicki Bock, Pat Butler, Fred and Kathy Cannataro, Laura Cooper, Carolyn Dameron, Kay Hein, Patti Digh-Howard, Dick Kiefer, Ken and Debbie Long, Sue Loos, Amy Love, Jonde Northcut, Grant Rorvick, Sharon Stensaas, Roger and Virginia Williams.

To the employees of Lewan & Associates who listened and responded with patience and helpful suggestions, we are indebted. Also the individuals who offered to provide an opening statement about the book are gratefully acknowledged. In addition, our sincere thanks to our many shipmates on Semester at Sea.

There are three others we feel we want to single out to thank for their special contributions in support of this work. We could not have done it without them: Linda Sue Shirkey, Jocelyn Billingsley, and Paul Lewan.

Foreword

I first met Lloyd Lewan in the spring of 1978 when I
inquired about a teaching position with Semester at Sea,
a program that takes 400-500 college students on a semester-
long, globe-circling educational odyssey. The man who
interviewed me for the position was the executive dean,
eventually to be my employer and close friend, Dr. Lloyd
S. Lewan. Lloyd had an office on campus, but he preferred
to talk to people with a mug of coffee in his hand at the
local pancake house. I met him there one bright, spring
afternoon. As I pulled up on my bicycle, I was greeted
by this great, bearded, bear of a man in a blue, button-
down dress shirt, no tie, white shorts, and tennis shoes.
I was later to discover that while on the ship this was his
uniform, the symbol of his informality and his accessibility.

Lloyd was not the same as the academic administrators
I had encountered before. He caught me completely by
surprise. He not only looked different, he talked differently. He spoke vividly, passionately, and with amazing
insight about a wide range of national and international

issues. He had the ability to penetrate to the heart of many complex problems and to explain them with marvelous clarity. I was later to see this same insight translated into effective action as I watched Lloyd guide the lives of over a thousand people on two of his many successful around-the-world voyages. Later I observed him use this identical range of insights and leadership skills with charitable and business enterprises conducted in the private sector. I watched him share his vision with a wide variety of enthusiastic audiences from civic to governmental and business arenas.

The conviction continually grew stronger in me that Lloyd's ideas deserved dissemination to a wider audience. This book, *Women in the Workplace: A Man's Perspective,* is a step in that direction. As you read it, I think you will find that his remarks carry a sense of authenticity that is undeniable. When you sit with Lloyd's audiences you hear them say: "Yes, that is so true. That really is my experience. That really is what happens!" The strength of his ideas is demonstrated by the fact that people continue to remember and discuss them weeks and even months later. The ideas are often disturbing, but they work. They really do illuminate and clarify much of our behavior, as you will see when you read this book and compare what it says with your own experience.

In simple yet powerful language, Lloyd explains why so many women are struggling with their jobs and why they work under conditions that make it difficult for them to gain full acceptance. As he does in his speeches, Lloyd develops an explanatory model and outlines the necessary steps that we must follow if we are to bring the sexes together in a more harmonious and productive fashion in the workplace.

Although the written word cannot hope to match the excitement and charisma of Lloyd's speeches, I have tried as much as possible to help Lloyd accurately render his vocal style. The book, like the man, stands on its own.

Ron Billingsley

Ron Billingsley

That is the great distinction between the sexes. Men see objects, women see the relationship between objects.

John Fowles, *The Magus*

Contents

Part I

A Place To Start

In the last thirty years sweeping economic and cultural changes have brought large numbers of female employees into the workplace. The U.S. Departments of Labor and Commerce report that since 1972 we have seen the addition of a million women each year to the labor force, from 33.5 million in 1972 to 47.7 million in 1982. Women now constitute over forty percent of the total labor force. Studies by the Bureau of Labor Statistics suggest that over sixty percent of all eligible women will be working by 1995. Perhaps of equal significance, "between 1950 and 1981 the labor force participation rate of mothers in the United States more than tripled." The change in the workplace has been steady and sustained throughout the entire century.

Yet we have not begun to make the kinds of adjustments that are necessary in order to use these new workers in ways that are fully satisfying to them and most effective for the institutions in which they choose to work. I do not need to spend your time here describing the frustration many women feel about the workplace and their ability to progress equally and fairly. This issue is constantly in front of us on the electronic media and in the press. This discontent is not healthy either for employees, male or female, or for employers. Facing this issue squarely will benefit both. Of equal importance, working on this challenge will contribute substantially to increasing harmony throughout our national life.

AS I SEE IT

There are certain fundamental attitudinal differences between the sexes that often make it very difficult for them to work well together.

AND

By acknowledging and understanding these basic attitudinal differences, professional effectiveness and economic equality can be greatly enhanced for the benefit of both men and women.

Men and women are not only clearly different physically, they are different in many other ways: the way they communicate, the way they handle power, the way they handle conflict, etc. There are great benefits to be derived from accepting this simple reality!

People, I believe, have always really understood this but for a variety of reasons do not want to talk about it in terms of what it means in the work environment. Unfortunately, all too often, these perceived differences have been used as an excuse to exploit and limit women in the workplace. What I hope to achieve in this book is to shed some light on this fascinating and important subject. First, let me say categorically that:

The sexes are equal, but different!

Much of the difficulty we experience today rests on our confusion about *difference* and *equality*. Different does not mean less valid, less significant, less entitled to equal opportunity. The sperm and the egg are very different, yet equally indispensible if new life is to begin. Greatly improved conditions in the workplace will be forthcoming when we come to fully appreciate that different does not mean unequal.

Speaking for myself I have to say: I don't want women to be like men! The world becomes a sad, desperate, and severely narrowed place when that happens. The sexes are designed to complement one another, to fit together. To ignore their complementary traits is to deny a fundamental truth and inevitably to create frustration. This is what is happening in many of our work environments today. We are expecting the sexes to behave in exactly the same ways, and we feel that to accept otherwise is to imply inferiority and/or favoritism.

3

We insist that both sexes perform in precisely the same way when what we should be doing is allowing each sex to behave in a way that utilizes its unique talents. As long as each sex is limited to the same methods and processes for achieving institutional excellence, we are restricting one or the other's capacity to design, develop, and help fully implement common institutional goals.

In this book I want to dwell on one of the most important and fundamental ways men and women are different, that is, in the *way* they deal with each other. I need to make it clear that when I say there are fundamental attitudinal differences, I am talking about the differences that most people, male and female, feel are inherent between the sexes.

Now you either agree with my assertion that the sexes are attitudinally different or you don't. In the following pages I intend to defend my point of view and demonstrate why acknowledging these differences makes sense and why it will benefit all of us irrespective of our sex. I do not expect you to accept everything I say in this book. But I challenge you to carefully consider the model presented and the examples that support it. I will follow these examples with suggestions that I think can help us improve the workplace for men and women.

TO MOVE ON . . .

Much should be said before attempting to offer a subject such as this, a man's perspective on women in the work-

4

place. Each of you who has chosen to think with me through these pages has many experiences of his/her own in the area of sex roles and work. Therefore, I will summarize and lead you quickly and directly into the heart of the message by a series of short, declarative statements that will serve as the foundation for what follows.

1. **Never in our work history have so many women needed or chosen to enter the work force.**

2. **This increasing percentage of women in the work force will continue into the 21st century.**

3. **Men and women have no formal training for working together, just as parents have no formal preparation for their crucial roles.**

4. **Men and women learn most of what they know about sex role behavior in their homes as children and in the social world of dating.**

5. **Armed mostly with these learned behaviors, men and women enter the work force and are asked immediately to perform as equals—it's not going to happen!**

6. **If we expect, ask for, or demand equal work competencies from men and women, then we must free the work environment from sex bias.**

7. We can free the workplace from sex bias when we are willing to acknowledge the different attitudinal tendencies that shape the behavior patterns of many men and women. Only then can an equal work environment emerge where competency is the sole criterion for success, salary, and promotion.

8. This perspective is offered NOW, for conditions that exist today. I recognize that things change and should change, hopefully for the better.

9. This is an American perspective and would not necessarily apply in other countries and cultures.

10. There are a few obvious limitations to my presentation of this issue.

   a. Most of what I offer is the result of years of my own measured, personal observations. This book is intended to be readable, practical, and fun. Readers with a greater or more scholarly interest in the subject should consult the many excellent source materials available in the field, some of which are included in the bibliography.

   b. This is a general concept, a fresh way to think about men and women in the workplace. It is designed to be a bit humorous and is certainly not offered as an angry model, which so often

6

is the posture adopted by men and women speaking on women's issues.

c. *PLEASE, Please, Please*, accept that I realize not all women and men fall into the tendencies described, and that my comments may at times be somewhat generalized and exaggerated in order to solidly make a point.

d. I have no intention of leaving the impression that all problems in the workplace between men and women are related entirely to sex role behavior. Obviously competence, leader behavior, work environment, and many other variables are critical as well.

e. I recognize that both men and women work for one or both of the following reasons: work for income - work for career. The model has different implications for each of these motives.

f. Many demographics, such as marital status, do affect the degree of applicability of this approach but do not significantly, in my judgment, invalidate the basic assertion. I speak to audiences that include teenagers, retired persons, married, divorced, and single persons, and the basic model seems to be acceptable to a wide range of people.

g. It is not the intent here to offer a prescription on how couples should structure their heterosexual relationships. Male-female relationships obviously represent a complex area of human interaction and one that is amenable to a variety of successful strategies.

h. I do not wish this book to, in any way, be construed as unappreciative of the thousands of capable, dedicated women who choose the role of mother and homemaker for all or periods of their work lives. For without such commitments families and society suffer.

11. My interest in presenting this subject is threefold:

a. I believe men control most working institutions, and it is time for more men to speak out in the area of sex roles in the workplace. Look at the bibliography. Most current books about gender roles and work are by women, and I do not think many men read them.

b. As a businessman I see the need to use all human talent and potential to the utmost. In my judgment, women represent the most under-utilized asset in the work force today.

c. I have made a personal commitment to help ensure that women's maximum talent is available to our institutions today.

Part II

The Model

I looked for a way to describe my experiences and my conclusions. The model offered here describes my findings and what I believe are the experiences of others. I have tested this model on dozens of mixed audiences, and the response has been general agreement.

Models are obviously limited, but the best of them provide new and effective ways to look at our experiences. I will call this model an "Acceptance Model." I think back to my years leading university and college students, faculty, and staff around the world on Semester at Sea. I stressed that the first step toward crosscultural understanding is acceptance. Acceptance should lead to understanding, which should lead to respect and then to appropriate interactions and actions. The goal for this book is to effect the first step in that same process, to bring men and women in the workplace to a higher degree of acceptance of the general attitude they have toward each other that affects the workplace. Hopefully they will then be willing to respect these differences and make some adjustments that would improve their interactions and ultimately improve their working environments.

Most of the attitudes we see in the workplace between men and women are a result of dating patterns and early childhood experiences.

WHAT DOES THIS MEAN?

Essentially, men objectify women.

Is this bad? I don't know, but that's the way it is. Men tend to see women more as physical objects than as relationships; men tend to be more interested in the object itself than in the relationship. *I am not saying that men are more objective than women,* i.e., that they are capable of more analytical and empirically based judgments. What I am saying is that men have the tendency to objectify people, and especially women. This is not a new phenomenon. We all objectify others to some extent. We objectify minorities, foreign "enemies," political opponents, etc. But the point here is that men particularly have a strong tendency to objectify.

Indeed, much of the energy of a private heterosexual relationship goes to modify this tendency to objectify.

But in the workplace energies must be directed toward the goals of the institutions and should not be siphoned off in frictional interpersonal encounters.

ON THE OTHER HAND . . .

Women are more interested in the quality of a relationship.

A sense of relationship demands the ability to commit, empathize, and have a reciprocal give-and-take connection with the other person. A good relationship between a man and a woman is one where both believe they significantly contribute to each other's growth or goals. There is a sense of responsibility between the two parties. There is true reciprocity. It is my contention that women generally do this better than men; they are generally more committed to relationship.

Why is this distinction important? Because when men and women come together in the workplace they operate from these sexually based perspectives. I believe that women and men have been heavily socialized in these behaviors by what they have witnessed in their homes and through dating.

Blue on boy babies, pink on girls . . .
Boys are made of snakes and snails . . .
Girls are . . . sugar and spice . . .
Behavior permitted boys is often denied girls . . .
Attitudes mothers and fathers display toward
    each other teach role patterns . . .
Who is expected to advance toward whom in dating . . .

And on and on.

My "acceptance" model asks that both parties respect these tendencies toward objectification and relationship in one another and move toward a "middle ground" where they can fully appreciate them in each other.

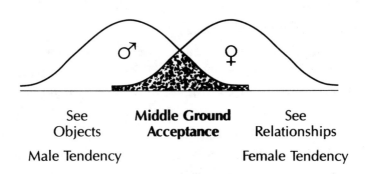

See	**Middle Ground**	See
Objects	**Acceptance**	Relationships
Male Tendency		Female Tendency

I also believe there are biological and genetic factors as well. Our bodies are "Incredible Machines," as one of the National Geographic Society's latest books so well documents. It concedes that we are in the "first stages of a genuine revolution in biology." I believe that it will be clear as the evidence pours in over the years that there are more and greater physiological and psychological differences between the sexes to be discovered.

The obvious sexually specific differences between men and women have been pointed out by many writers and may be summarized as: Men have genitals on the outside of their bodies. Women are protected genitally. Men need to be aroused to engage in reproductive activity whereas women do not. Women bear children; women breast feed and men do not.

Chemical differences have been traced, examined, and reported as well. The most noteworthy is the male hormone—testosterone—which is believed to be the basis for male aggressive behavior.

Neuroscientists are discovering some limited information on how male and female brain hemispheres operate. The observations include differences in brain electrical activity as men and women perform various tasks. Women's brains may be less specialized and have better integration and communication between the two major brain hemispheres. It has been further suggested that women and men use the same sides of their brains for different purposes.

Sustained research, I think, will continue to show that nurturing and relationship are more natural to a female. I willingly concede, however, that despite all the scientific evidence to suggest biological differences, socialization is still a dominant influence in the development of sex role behavior for men and women. It is not so important to me to discuss why men and women are different as to reflect on what these differences mean in the workplace *now!*

Whatever the reasons, these attitudinal differences prevail:

Men Objectify Women

Women Emphasize Relationship

In *The Cinderella Complex: The Price Women Pay*, Colette Dowling asks:

> "Do women fear independence or do they really resist giving up relationship?"

This is the agenda we're dealing with. Let's be honest and get it on the table where we can all see it and deal with it.

In the conduct of my examination of the literature for this book I was heartened by the discovery of the following quotes:

From *Breaking Into the Boardroom*, by Jinx Melia:

Many of the women who are not using sexuality are busy trying to regulate it away by creating a third sex— the professional. She is often an unknowing female variation of a eunuch: a member of the opposite sex who can toil without risk among the virile. But unless we are willing to become like machines, we have to recognize there is no third sex. We can either act like men, or act like women—or combine the skills of both. If we refuse to act like either one, we end up with nothing.

From *Women of Tomorrow*, by Kathy Heaton, President of *Omni Magazine:*

My dream for tomorrow's woman is not that she become like man but that she influence the future with her own intellect, values and perceptions.

And finally from *On Your Own Terms*, by Kathryn Stechert:

The high value women place on caring can lead them to include concern for interpersonal relationships when confronted with an issue or problem. Men, who are more externally oriented toward a project or goal, tend not to weigh the effects of alternative solutions on relationships.

15

To women such as these authors and to many others, I owe a great deal. Their wisdom and forthrightness have given me the courage to address this complex issue of women at work from a man's perspective.

Part III

The Defense of the Model

I don't expect you to accept these assertions just because I make them. So I am going to give you as many examples as I can, outlined in four loosely defined areas.

1. **Intimacy**
2. **Family Life**
3. **Daily Living**
4. **The Workplace**

I recognize that personal experiences vary between individuals and that these examples are drawn from a wide variety of life experiences as I've seen them or had them shared with me. *Choose only those you can identify with as you attempt to value what I am suggesting herein.*

INTIMACY

Maybe Mother Was Right . . . All Men Are The Same When It Comes To Intentions Toward Women!

Emotional Patterns in Dating

In the initial phases of a relationship with a woman, males are generally very attentive, very thoughtful, and very affectionate. This pattern of attentiveness will remain until the relationship has become stabilized. Women say, "You were so charming when we first met, so gentle and thoughtful. What happened?" Indeed, what happens to the male's emotional intensity after he has secured the desired object?

Males tend to be most attentive when they are trying to attract their object. You might say they are predators—perhaps a crass description but I think fundamentally accurate.

What is the intensity pattern of a woman's emotional growth in a relationship? A woman builds more slowly. The intensity of involvement develops gradually until, all of a sudden, she concludes, "Hey, this is a super person! This is a nice guy; I like him and what he is about." It is at this point that her emotional intensity quickly and powerfully accelerates. And just about then, what's happening to the male's intensity? Yes! It is falling off because he has, in one sense or another, secured the object.

And this is what happens in most heterosexual relationships. The woman gets to a point of real intensity, a point where she commits to the relationship. The woman's sense of the significance of relationship compels her toward commitment. And unfortunately, at this point of greatest possibility for the relationship, the male's intensity often diminishes with the cry, "You're smothering me."

This is the situation that provokes the equally intense cry one hears so often from women, "I'm tired of playing games!" Yet if the emotional patterns that distinguish men from women that I have outlined here truly exist, women and men really do not have much choice. It really need not be viewed as a game, if both are prepared to accept this reality and make adjustments.

A Marriage Commitment Tends To Offset This Tendency Toward Great Emotional Fluctuation In Men.

Dating Ads

You have only to pick up any local newspaper that permits personal dating ads, and you will quickly see the distinction I am trying to make in this book. Most females searching for male contact use words that emphasize relationship and romance. I have read hundreds of "personals." The female ads used over and over again such words and phrases as: "companionship, . . . wish to share beliefs and interest, . . . seek mutual interest in, . . . enjoy blazing fires and candlelight, . . . love and affection, . . .

19

must be caring and supportive, . . . seek lasting relationship," etc., etc. Many end with the warning, "Those interested in purely physical relationships need not apply." Females will often add some of their own physical characteristics at the end, especially age and weight; they know it is necessary.

Male ads often first spell out the great attributes of the writer. "Tall, strong, professional male," and then the real objectives follow. "Seeks noontime rendezvous with female of any color—single or married, fat women a turn-off."

Two such ads read on the day I edited this page are quoted below as printed.

SWM (Single White Male - for those of you who don't read these ads)

Very Handsome SWM 36, 6'2", 195, light brown hair, blue eyes, muscular build, well-educated, very successful professional, non-smoker, non-drug user, social drinker. Loves adventure, travel, outdoors and fine living. Seeking slender, attractive lady, 21- 35, photo appreciated.

Attention: Affectionate Female 48, 5'8", 125 lbs. Would like to meet male who has good self-esteem, high priorities for human potential, wants to share sense of humor and spirit for living.

Pick up the "personals" and see for yourself. Dating services, personal ads, singles' establishments, and all the rest tell us: Yes, men and women both search for each other, but I still believe that the motivation *at first* is subtly different.

Men First Seek A Woman, Women First Seek A Relationship

Dial a conversation

The latest fad to sweep America (which may be made illegal) is the ads that urge you to dial a charge number and hear live conversation. Some that I saw read:

Talk to 3 women
Listen in on women talking,
Earth tones.
Female form, live for men by women.
Soft and tender.
Outlaw phone, live talk.

I confess I checked a few out. It is primarily women, for men to talk to, with the exception of homosexual ads. I believe women would rather have intimate conversations with men they care about, not strangers.

Describing the Opposite Sex

How do most men in this society describe women? If one man calls up another one and says "I got you a date for tomorrow night," how will the caller describe the woman to his friend? Yes, most of the time he will give a physical description first. "She's tall, she's dark-haired, she's thin . . ." and then maybe what she does and what activities she enjoys. If the caller doesn't describe her, he will be asked to, you can be sure.

Now, how do you think most women in a similar situation would describe a potential date to a girlfriend? "He's intelligent, educated, fascinating; has done a lot of interesting things; traveled extensively; has worked on such and such a project. He believes strongly in . . ." She might add if pressed, "He's a little overweight and has a beard that's graying and he's losing his hair." Females don't think so much in objectifying terms. They think of the possibilities for relationship. It is the potential character and quality of that relationship that they will present to the other person first, then in a more subtle fashion, they will add physical characteristics.

How many times have you heard someone say, "I don't know what she sees in him." We have all seen some extremely lovely women going around with some pretty average looking men. Why? The relationship is good. Women will generally be happy with most physical circumstances if the quality of the person and the relationship are good. Having said all that, I know women still notice handsome or physically attractive men. But that is what women *see*—they *want* more. Maybe another way to say all of this is: *Women see men as eligible, men see women as available.*

On Parade

I have a female friend in her late twenties who was recently invited by a very distinguished gentleman to lunch at his private club. The members of the club were mostly prominent business executives, and they were having a special lunch to which each of them invited a woman friend to meet the other members. They had a nice social hour and then they ate lunch. The women were encouraged to sit with a person other than the one who brought them. I asked my friend to "describe the women and describe the men, in general." She replied, "The men were an average group, some thin, some fat, some bald, some handsome." I prodded: Describe the women. "All young, thin, and gorgeous." Now if you turned it around and it was a women's club having the same kind of activity, what would the men look like? If you think about it for even a moment, you know. The women are more likely to invite the most *interesting* men they could find, not necessarily the most physically attractive.

In most social situations on college campuses, which women are usually the last approached? Are they the women who fit the ideal American pattern of beauty? No. They are usually less attractive, physically. Is that an objectification of women? Of course. Does a woman work that way? No. Most women are willing to talk to someone who is interesting, nice, and respectful of them. Physical appearance is not all that important to them. What women see is the quality of a person, the possibility of a relationship. What would our world be like if this were not so,

23

if women had the same tendency toward objectification that men have?

Weekends Away

In our society men and women like to spend weekends away. Imagine that a man asks a woman to go to Lake Tahoe for the weekend. What must she assume? Her assumption without further explanation must be that she is agreeing to intimacy. A far better way to handle this request on the part of a male who wanted quality time would be: "Would you consider going to Lake Tahoe with me this weekend? Separate rooms (beds), no intimate expectations. I just want to spend quality time with you." *Negotiate Intimacy, Don't Assume It.*

Sexuality

Sexually, it seems to me, women have to be connected emotionally. Men can read manuals on the techniques and technology of "good sex" forever and it won't do them half as much good as a context of genuine tenderness and affection. This is because the sexuality is not primarily physical and technical, it's emotional and intellectual; it's a matter of communication and relationship. Sexuality to a woman is the natural extension of a good relationship. Most women know this, at least intuitively. So they seem more compelled to talk, to shape the sex act into a form of true relationship if they can. The female is usually much more responsive, much more interested in sexuality when there has been an intimate and complete connection with the male on nonphysical levels. This is why women

24

are often baffled at the speed with which men can rush toward intercourse. To many men, sex is an objective activity that satisfies an objective "need." For most women there is no great hurry because intercourse is simply the final, and hopefully the most beautiful, expression of a legitimate relationship. And all that precedes intercourse is not merely preamble, but a delightfully varied expression of that same sense of intimacy, caring, and relationship. To illustrate this I ask you: who needs tenderness *after* the sex act as much as or more than before, men or women? Who likes to hug and kiss most, men or women? Most audiences immediately respond almost unanimously, "Women!"

What this boils down to in terms of exchanges between the sexes is a motivational difference. Although they both may want intimacy on some level, the motives that compel men and women toward intimacy may be different. If the motives are different, then invariably the strategies for arriving at intimacy will be different. Naturally this difference in motive and style can be the source of great confusion, misunderstanding and of course, disharmony.

Softer Things

Who is more appreciative of the little acts of tenderness, thoughtfulness, gentleness, politeness in families, at work, and in general—women or men? My audiences respond, "Women!" Because these are primarily *relational* acts. Are these attributes that women like in men? Absolutely! It has been said, "Women use sex to get affection, men use affection to get sex."

5 to 1 Rule

My years of observation tell me without question that a man, any man, old or young, handsome or plain, rich or poor, smart or dull, successful or unsuccessful, can keep a good woman loving him simply by showing continuous signs that he values the relationship—flowers, walks, holding hands, cuddling, thank-you notes under the pillow, postcards while on the road, a kiss on the neck while his wife or woman is doing something for him, special acknowledgment of her with surprise gifts, an unexpected dinner out, turning off the TV to talk, going to activities and places important to her, etc. The only hitch is that in my judgment, a woman entering a new relationship ought to wait for at least five such acts of relationship before she believes that he too is interested in commitment. And even when she does believe, she should then only take one step toward a man. I guess I mean . . .

Walk, don't run, ladies, toward relationship if you want to survive a man.

Aging

Gray hair on a man is distinguished, on a woman, it's aging. Women let men age, for they see more than the physical aspects of a man. Men tend not to allow women to age gracefully because they are more occupied with their physical aspects.

Men are more valued and women less valued as they age in our society.

I recently dated a woman who said, "You're so handsome, your face has character lines." No, I don't, I have wrinkles. She says, "You're so strong." No I'm not, I'm flabby. What does she see? She doesn't see only an object, she sees my character. She sees what I think about; she sees what I believe in, and that is mainly what she values. She accepts my body as part of all that. Men don't accept an aging woman as easily.

Balding

If a husband is balding, what will most wives do? Tell their husbands that bald is handsome, distinguished, and most of all that it makes no difference to her.

What would a man do if his wife went bald? You tell me, but I will bet *my* money that *his* money would be down on a wig, fast!

The Double Standard

We have all heard about the "double standard" in sexuality. Does it exist? You bet! The double standard is alive and well in American society. What do I mean by that? Are women more forgiving of men who are less than faithful? Yes, I think so. This does not mean that they will ever accept infidelity, but they might forgive it. When? When the relationship is good. Women know that men are capable of getting "sidetracked" by many different women without the pretext of a committed relationship. Should women be forgiving? Perhaps not, but where would many men be if they were not? Don't misunderstand, she will forgive, *not forget*, because she is concerned with preserving a relationship and thus can forgive more behaviors.

Now, can you find as many males who are forgiving of sexual infidelity? I don't know many men who would be very forgiving if their wife or woman friend decided to have an affair with another man. How many men you know would accept their female partner coming home and saying, "I hate to have to admit this, but I just spent the weekend with John." Would he be able to put it in perspective like a woman? Probably not. Most would neither forgive nor forget. Accept, maybe.

Perhaps I should add here that the reason men are so unforgiving is that they instinctively know that when a woman, who is naturally relational, seeks another man, her allegiance to them is shattered. Even in today's era of modern sexuality most women do not easily stray from their primary sexual partner.

When Women Leave

Women tend only to leave men when the relationship is tested, tried, and proven to no longer be of value and meaning. Except of course, sadly, when economics force them to stay.

Jealousy

Men don't do well when their woman partner is pursued by other men. Why?

Men are only jealous of one thing. Other men!

They objectify women, and they don't like any other men near the woman they care about. They don't even like "their woman" going to lunch with other men. Dozens of women that I have talked to over the years report, "My husband gets uptight because I have lunch with another man." No matter how innocent the relationship, males are generally jealous of males.

What are women jealous of? Everything that detracts from their relationship.

That could be the Chicago Bears, TV activity, beer-drinking buddies, mothers-in-law, hunting, sleeping, anything that detracts from the relationship. Obviously there are exceptions. But if you examine the pattern I think you will find it holds true.

Healing Relationship

In tough times who initiates talk to find out what is happening with any male-female relationship? Men or women? My audiences invariably respond, "The women!"

Ask the married couples you know. Who initiates most conversations when there is a problem? What I usually hear is "My wife wants to talk about everything." Men talk a lot as a catharsis, getting something off their chest. But this is not what women want. They want feedback! That's reciprocal and relational.

29

Trust Me

Who is more likely to say, "Trust me" in personal situations? Women respond quickly during my talks, "Men." I asked one distinguished woman in an audience why she felt this to be so. She replied simply, "Women don't have to say it, they constantly show or demonstrate it. Trust is a natural part of relationship."

Clearing the Air

Imagine something happening in the relationship between a man and a woman. The relationship is in trouble. Some act occurs that is causing friction between the partners. When the trouble hits, whatever it is, they talk, usually initiated by the woman, and they decide that the situation is cleared up. If you are primarily a relational person, that means "it's clear." You push the "clear" button and dismiss it. Now, males will say, "yes, we are clear." However, six months later, when something else comes up what may a male do? He may go way back into that storage bank and find every one of those things that went wrong in the last five years and haul them out, clouding up today's issue. Why? He will store things up and bring those things out when he wants to win or punish—a form of objectification. A female, who is more committed to a relationship, can more easily dispense with the transgressions of the past, so long as they no longer impinge on today's relationship. Women, however, *will* dredge up the past if it is the same problem and there has been "backsliding" or "more of the same."

Two Intimate Relationships at Once

In a recent talk I gave to a large group of federal employees I asked, "Who can more comfortably juggle two intimate relationships at the same time?" You guessed it, the audience thundered, "Men!" I have never read of a woman having two families, one in Detroit and the other in San Francisco. Have you? Polygamy in history seems of greater interest to men.

Open Relationships

I listened to a friend over dinner a few months ago, and she told me her man wanted to "change" their relationship to a noncommitted basis. It would be "healthier." The ground rule was that they could both date others. She objected but ultimately gave in. After her first "other" date, he called, wanted all the details, and behaved very jealously. He wanted it both ways, no relationship but a relational woman.

Dating and Children

When men date women with children, the women seem to keep all the relationships going, *hers* with the man, *hers* with her children, *hers* with his children. In other words, she does it all.

A woman friend of mine with children was recently married. He too had children. She admitted to me that,

"We've had a lot of problems with the boys adjusting to each other." When I asked her how her husband handles it she said, with what I felt was honesty, "He's oblivious to it all."

Women will assume relational responsibilities, and men know it.

Remarriage

More often than not, the motivation for a second marriage fits the same pattern of behavior I have been describing.

A woman wants a new relationship, a man wants a new object.

A very successful businessman colleague of mine always tells me that if his wife died, he would have to find a companion or he would never make it. His wife agrees and encourages him to think like that. She on the other hand, always says, "I can't think about remarrying because I have the best relationship a woman could ever want." Would she marry again? I think so, but it would have to be a good relationship. Women can live on the memories of a good relationship and fall back on the strength of other relationships they have established in life—children, friends, etc.

FAMILY

Household Dynamics

If I were to ask you, "Who was the head of the household where you were raised, your father or your mother (assuming both were present)? Chances are that you would say, "Well, my father was the assumed head of the household." In most traditional American families people would say that the father, at least in a titular sense, was the head of the household. Now . . . if I asked you, "Who was the glue?" That's right—Mom! Working or nonworking mom, it makes no difference. All audiences responded the same, all the time. The father may be the head of the household, but the mother is the real glue that holds the family together. She is more relational. She has the relationship with the kids, she has the relationship with the in-laws, with the neighbors, with the animals, the plants, with the teachers, etc. *Why?* Because women are better human beings? No, but because they respect and nurture relationships. After all, relationship is what family is all about.

Visiting the Family

Who feels more obligated to visit families on vacations? I bet on women.

Hugging, Kissing, Touching

Hugging, kissing, and touching were invented by women. I have said to many audiences that the first sign of a changing marriage or relationship is when the man stops hugging and kissing. Kissing, when not a conscious prelude to sex, is *really* relational.

Protectionism

Men are generally more protective of their wives, sisters, daughters, mothers, than of their brothers, sons or fathers. They know other males; they know those males will objectify these women like most others. Therefore they instinctively move to prevent that. They do not want their sister or daughter or mother getting "hit on" by another man.

The Price Men Pay

I have observed that because women are so central to relationships men often experience a sense of loneliness in a family unit. They sometimes feel left out and insignificant. This is further accentuated by their less-developed abilities to express and communicate feelings. Especially after a divorce, men may feel left out of a real relationship with their children. It is hard for them to do it alone. I always ask my nieces and nephew to call me "Uncle Lloyd," rather loudly, so I am not lumped with all those divorced fathers trying so hard with their children at MacDonalds on any Friday evening. I feel sad for these men as they work at the unfamiliar task of building relationships in the brief and intermittent periods they have.

Husbands As Friends

Recently I was watching one of the major network TV interview programs—Oprah Winfrey, I believe—and I remember clearly someone said, "Women talk more to women about important things than to their husbands." I wanted to shout, "This doesn't have to be!" My brother proudly proclaims that his wife is his best friend. But all too often a woman needs "other" best friends and confidants to talk about things she is not able to discuss with her husband.

Adopting Children

Who is the one who generally provides the motivation for adoption? Who feels most unfulfilled without children? I cannot help but believe that women provide that motivation and most strongly crave the joy of children. I continue to believe that women are the creators of relationship, especially those with children, and are most prepared to make the necessary commitment. Men prefer to create an offspring and leave a legacy and enjoy them, as long as there is someone else to handle the day-to-day requirements of children.

Family Fun

Recently I attended a family water-recreation park. Waiting in a long line, where people were close together, generally in bathing suits, my female companion and I counted over fifty men and women who passed close to us. All but six of the men looked at my companion in a male way—the "body look." The women also looked at my companion, but we felt it was to compare suits and to guess at our relationship. Not one woman looked at me. Obviously these behaviors might be due to my body versus hers, but I don't think so. My point is, even out with the family, women are viewed as sexual objects by passing men.

Discipline

Who is the disciplinarian in most homes? Papa is supposed to be, but who is the real disciplinarian that imposes order and standards, daily and consistently? Dad may administer the spanking or whatever punishment is the end result of poor behavior but mother is the real disciplinarian who, hour after hour and day after day, defines and enforces the rules. And this is inevitable, even if the father works around the house, because discipline is a part of any relationship.

Watch the behavior of a family unit in a restaurant. Who handles the children, unless the woman demands otherwise? Mom! Men help of course, but intercede especially if they are embarrassed by a child's behavior or if interrupted. In the family, discipline is contingent on caring. On some level of consciousness, children know this. They will continue to misbehave until they force you to *prove* that you care enough to discipline them. Women, it seems to me, are better at consistently caring about discipline as they know it helps children.

Having Children

Having recently served as birth coach for a wonderful seventeen-year-old mother, I listened to instructions given in preparatory classes about the need to be especially careful of male partners feeling left out. I began to realize that even in conjugal relationships men sometimes have difficulty understanding that having a child extends the relationship, indeed is part of the union with the woman, and offers another possible form of connectedness for both parents. Some men may experience feelings that babies are an intrusion on the time and attention they receive from their primary relational object.

Divorce

I have done a fair amount of divorce counseling, and the cry of women is often "he won't talk to me." Who do you think most wants to go for counseling in divorce situations? That's right, the women. Why? Because they want to talk about it, they want to make a stab at preserving the relationship. It's a commitment they made, and if it's a commitment, they are willing to work on it. Relationships demand commitment. Women are willing to go into counseling if the relationship is worth saving, and they try to bring the men along if they can.

Many women also say to me, "The real sadness of my marriage breakup was that I never knew what went wrong, what happened." Many years ago I left my own wife with no real explanation of what went wrong. I am sorry to this day.

Males don't share feelings easily and tend to say very little when feelings are deteriorating toward a woman. I find one of two events has to occur before a man will take decisive action toward leaving a woman. Either he finds another woman or he becomes convinced that he does not want the present woman anymore. In these cases little valuable communication takes place. The relationship just disintegrates, and generally women are left hanging. Women on the other hand will divorce or leave a man when the relationship deteriorates to an unacceptable level, and often reluctantly.

Child Custody

Who is most often awarded the custody of children in a divorce proceeding? Even our social and judicial systems acknowledge that women generally are more natural at family unit maintenance. I know this is changing, but only a "smidgen."

If the situation were reversed, do you think women would default on child support payments the way men have since the 1960s? I think not.

Post-Divorce Relationships

I find that women try harder to maintain some kind of relationship even after the marriage has ended, often for the sake of the children, but also because of the investment they have made in the person while the relationship was good.

I have been amazed at the number of men who simply want to ignore their ex-wives, even if the children suffer. Again, there are many exceptions and some divorced fathers work hard at maintaining openness with ex-wives for the sake of the children. But, women still do it best . . .

Survival

Women seem to survive better without men, in every way. They seem to have more personal power, the ability to fill the void of a lost companion with other friends and family. They are emotionally sturdier than men. They seem to live beyond primary relationships. Nursing homes tell the story; they are mainly filled with women.

On a personal level, my father died in a relatively short period after he was separated from his wife, even though he was with my brother and me. I have always felt that this was due in some measure to her absence. She was the main person he had been with for years. My step-mother is still alive, many years later.

DAILY LIVING

Same-Sex Friendships

You go to any local hangout in the downtown area of a big city and locate two women sharing an evening meal together. What will you observe? Intensely animated conversation, eye contact, interested looks. Women have great friendships. Women really talk to one another. They have committed relationships in which there is deep personal sharing. For example, the popular TV police show, *Cagney and Lacey* (two women detectives), is equally about a relationship and detective work.

I do not mean to suggest here that men do not also have good friendships. But there is a profound difference. If you see two men together who are friends, most of the time there will be an activity involved or a discussion of work, sports, or other "things." There has to be an activity, a thing to show or share: fishing, hiking, golf. Men go to ball games; they work on the car. Feelings and intimacies are funneled, when they are shared at all, through the medium and jargon of the activity, rather than in a direct, intimate, relational way.

The reticence of men to express affection for one another in a physical way, except in some kind of very macho environment like a football field, is another example of their general difficulty with relationship. Relationship involves a connection between people that is naturally expressed physically as well as verbally. Men express feelings indirectly and ambiguously through a shared activity. In this way they can feel protected from their sense of unsureness about how to express affection and from their fear of direct intimacy.

It requires a real stretching of the personality for most men to alter this pattern. Men just don't develop personal support systems with other men as well as women do with each other, and men's support systems are very often women!

"Hopeful" Contact

Men, if you doubt my analysis of male/female tendencies, go test it for yourself as I do. Go to a major supermarket and walk up and down the aisles, trying to catch the eyes of women. What you will invariably find is that it is almost impossible to get sustained eye contact with a woman. Why is that? No context.

An attractive woman may be prey to dozens of male eyes as she waits for her groceries to be checked out. Males, at best, will get a subtle peek from women waiting in line or walking around the store. Women know that your eye contact alone has nothing to do with relationship. How could it? You are only there for fifteen minutes picking up peanut butter.

I notice when jogging or walking on my daily exercise rounds that I can hardly catch a female's eye anywhere. They only speak when spoken to and very carefully. They do not normally extend the greeting—no context. Women only warm up to me on my walks as they see me over and over again, for then they begin to feel safe, making a judgment that my walking is indeed for improved health.

On the contrary, men are very bold in their eye contact. A passing *derriere* can rob them of their focus on fitness. Males respond to objects. As I drive my jeep around and come to stoplights, I notice that mostly men look into cars to their left and right to see if there is a female to look at who just might show interest. Female hitchhikers are picked up almost immediately by men. (Not true for male hitchhikers.) Ask yourself why—hopeful contact!

Magazines

The next time you are in the grocery store, browse the magazines at the checkout stand that are designed mainly for women. Look at *Redbook, Cosmopolitan, New Woman,* and others. The feature articles are often focused on relational items. For example, a recent cover of *Woman* magazine contained all of the following titles:

The Gentle Art of Talking To Each Other In Bed

'I'M GETTING TIRED OF ACCEPTING THE RELATIONSHIP ON HIS TERMS'

BUILDING A MARRIAGE THAT HAS STAYING POWER
(And Will Thrive Through The Ebb And Flow Of Love)

You're In Love With A Married Man—And That Man Is Your Boss . . .
BITCHINESS CAN BE BEAUTIFUL
And Get You What (Or Who) You Want

These are hardly saleable subjects in men's magazines. If you examined a current issue of *M: The Civilized Male*, you would find:

Dream Jobs And the Men Who Have Them

Wall Street's Man in Washington

Wine Wizards

South Seas Headhunters

The Hottest Cars Are His Routines

A look at other male magazines, *GQ, Esquire*, etc., would reveal almost identical subject matter. It seems to me that the strong differences in gender orientation is clearly revealed by these examples of popular reading matter.

Spiritual Men

Many women seem to respond to spiritual men because they feel that such a man is truly capable of a relationship, because relationship with God requires reciprocity, commitment, and of course, service. *My experience is that a mutually acceptable spiritual basis for any relationship provides the strongest foundation and promise.*

Adjustments in any Relationship

Who makes most of the adjustments in the majority of male/female relationships, i.e., personal, work, family? Women! They seem to value the relationship more than men do and will make the necessary adjustments more readily, even to the extent of giving up or reprioritizing their own needs. Perhaps this has a lot to do with the increasing divorce rate. Are women less willing to make all the adjustments today?

Abstinence

You answer this one. Who seems more able to handle long periods of time without intimacy with the opposite sex, men or women? Women, because without a relationship to encompass the intimacy it isn't as important. This in no way is intended to suggest that women do not have sexual needs equivalent to males, only greater self-control and preference for context.

Anger

When deceit, however slight, comes up between a man and woman as part of their relationship, who is more likely to use anger to hide the associated guilt or to avoid a frank discussion? Again, my audience response supports my view that men clearly do so. Or when a man gets caught flirting by his wife, is he more likely to use anger or apologize?

Advertising

This is yet another powerful example of the fact that males tend to objectify women and women buy into it. Turn on the television or pick up a magazine and you can immediately see that much modern advertising is geared to getting men to crave products through their favorite objects—females. Either that or advertising is trying to get women to objectify themselves so that they can be more desirable to men.

Calvin Klein jeans provocatively displayed on young women, or a Midol ad with a nude woman showing areas of menstrual discomfort, or a Pampers ad with the mother in a sensual nightgown holding up what appears to be a recently changed baby represent successful examples of this strategy. I will concede that there are exceptions, and needed changes are coming to this practice.

Who Can Be Conned, Who Can Be Manipulated?

Who is more easily conned? Women, I think. Why? They *want* to believe. A man can tell a woman he loves kids and she assumes he would be interested in her children or in having his own. Not necessarily. This may only be part of his approach.

I freely admit, men can be manipulated by women through appeals to their pride, their sense of importance, their symbols. One woman manipulated me to a gathering by saying, "I know all the people at the party are just dying to meet *you* since you are so well known to most of them as a superb speaker." I went!

45

Volunteerism

This is a concept generally maintained by women. Why? Because in the absence of a commercial work arrangement they can be useful. But I believe it is also because women are more sensitive to the relational basis of community. They know that most nonprofit agencies are helping people and families, so they volunteer.

Police

It seems to me that male police officers more easily objectify wrongdoers as "bad" and seek to deal with them peremptorily as a category when situations are confrontational. I believe women officers are prone to use more relational strategies in confrontational situations.

Music

Most popular music is a social commentary, some of it addressing the issue of male/female relationships. I awoke early one morning to a male voice singing these words.

"Baby, Baby, don't get hooked on me, because I'll use you then I'll set you free."

Homosexuality in Society

Do men or women better accept homosexuality in society and in their children? Who establishes better relationships with declared homosexuals? I would have to say women. Why? Because relationship is a total thing and sexual preference is only one part of a whole person, not great enough to warrant rejecting a relationship that is on the whole meaningful.

Pornography

Is pornography male or female? Who creates it? What does it do? It generally objectifies women and sometimes, even worse, children. Even where you see women going to the currently fashionable male strip joints, do they go because they really want to drool over an object? Generally women go to these places with a group of friends. They go because it is a matter of curiosity and perhaps independence; it is worth a few laughs. Maybe it is even a good way to prove a point.

Males are different. They are attracted to the object without a context. You seldom find women in X-rated bookstores paying 25 cents to see a one-minute dirty movie. And not because women are prohibited, inhibited, or would be assaulted, but because pornography is objective, without context, and really not of serious, ongoing interest to women. Secondly, if you attend a "blue" movie theater in any modern American city, you often find it divided by choice into two sections, "men" and "couples." Once I asked a frequent visitor to a theater of this type, "Where's the female section?" He laughed uproariously and said, "It would be empty."

For most women, sexual intimacy with a man has to have a context. Pornography and XXX movies don't do

47

it because there is no context of relationship. And though I could never prove it, I'll bet men produce most pornography that exists today. "Honk if you're horny" bumper stickers don't fit the feminine nature.

Prostitution

First, let me say I know most men don't want prostitutes, but nonetheless only men use prostitutes. How many male prostitutes, other than homosexual ones, do you think we have in this country? I don't know. Does it matter? No, but the real question is, why are most prostitutes women? Because men are capable of driving down the street, picking up a woman, quickly performing a specific act, and then moving on, no context or relationship necessary. Prostitutes can use this male tendency of objectification for what they perceive as their advantage. My interviews with prostitutes confirm that men are interested in a particular activity, clearly defined. They are not interested in a relationship of any kind with that woman. They also confirm that, as one said, "All kinds of men pick me up, businessmen, professional men, construction workers, married and single, all types."

There are indeed male "gigolos" or companions for women. But why gigolos or companions? What do they do? They purport to give a woman a relationship.

Violence

I watch television and read major newspapers and I find that women can be driven to violence as well as men.

But I submit that if you review most reported violent acts committed by women they tend to be around relational problems or situations. Women aren't shooting at others on freeways in California for no apparent reason or shooting someone over an exchange of insults outside a bar. I would even go one step further and suggest that if you read about women involved in major crimes, they seem to be involved with a man in that crime.

Rape

We read and hear that rape is a crime of violence, not sex. I have no quarrel with this, but what is essential to this book is the fact that it is a *male act*. Only men can take pleasure in such a dastardly act. Rape represents the ultimate low of the objectification perspective.

"Date rape" seems a particularly striking example of the male capacity to react to a woman as an object. Why should anyone continue to press another person against her/his strenuous objections, regardless of who went out with whom and in whose apartment they are? *No is no*!

War

How often have I heard, "if it were up to women there would be no wars." Of course, relationships demand alternative, less extreme, less violent solutions to problems. It is so much easier to get men to objectify enemies and then to fight them. I would even go so far as to suggest that if women led all nuclear nations on earth, there would be a speedier, more committed path to the reduction of nuclear weapons. The results of nuclear war are unacceptable to women's relational nature.

Jinx Malia seems to agree when she remarks in her book, *Breaking Into the Boardroom*,

> "Generally speaking, women can negotiate better than they can fight. Our role is not as warrior, but as peacemaker; not in the Army but in the State Department; not on the battlefield but at the treaty conference table."

THE WORKPLACE

> And sex is perhaps the most important of personal characteristics. Even though sex may have nothing to do with the job or task at hand, it is far from irrelevant to the workplace.
>
> Kathryn Stechert, *On Your Own Terms*

Interviewing

I observed a young male manager interviewing twelve candidates for a position. Eleven were women. He consistently, without realizing it, spent five to ten extra minutes with the attractive women, as contrasted to the man or less attractive females. *Men, we must be more aware of our actions that are sexually biased.*

Language

I heard a salesman say to a new saleswoman co-worker, "You'll do fine, you're better looking than I am." Men, those kinds of statements just signal women that you are viewing them as objects, not as talent.

Sexual Harassment

Studies I have read over the years reveal that an amazingly high percentage of women report being sexually harassed on the job. How accurate such studies are is hard to assess. But what is significant to this book is that there is not a similar body of research showing such sexual harassment of men by women. It doesn't even occur to anyone to conduct such research. We know it is unneeded.

Don't Send Me Women

I recently overheard a male manager of a mechanical repair unit say to his personnel department, "Don't send me women mechanics. They stir up the troops." What else can I say?

Women in Sales

As a senior player in a large office products dealership, representing major equipment lines including computer equipment and supplies, I learned the value of relationship at work from women salespersons. As electronic equipment became more sophisticated and moved from box sales to value-added system sales, trust and commitment to customers became increasingly important. We saw that hard work in the interest of customers was vital to sales, equal to or even more important than price. Guess what we simultaneously discovered? Women often do this better than men, and we are adding women to our sales force with enthusiasm.

Is this to say that men aren't capable of sensitive and highly developed relationships with customers? Of course not. But here is an example of how women's unique abilities can be of special value. Why we resist accepting this is the only question.

Dress at Work

If I see one more woman in a pin-stripe suit, with a thing that looks like a tie, I am going to wear a dress.

Let women be women and dress accordingly, not like men. Professional dress is professional dress for a man or a woman. Women should not have to conform to masculine concepts of color and style in order to appear professional. Let them be classy and professional in their own way.

Display of Emotion

I hear men in the workplace say, "Women are too emotional!" Have you heard that? What do men mean when they say that? They don't know how to deal with displays of emotion. In effect the woman is asking them to be relational, which can seem like unsafe ground to many men.

What does a relationship demand? Openness, honesty, vulnerability. It demands one who shares her or his inner feelings and one who is thus more likely to be outwardly emotional. Women tend to show emotion because it is a statement about the relationship, even at work. *Women are different, not difficult.*

What is at issue here, of course, is not only display of emotion in the workplace, but who will display it, when and why. Surely men are capable of displaying the same kinds of emotion as women but they are not conditioned to do so. Nor are they expected to do so. Men don't react or show emotion, other than anger. *I think emotion is OK for men or women.*

In *The New Executive Woman*, Marcille G. Williams says, "Whatever you do, don't cry . . . in the long run it will endanger your careers." No! Why make women change, let men accept.

Getting Involved at Work

As more men and women work together, there will invariably be more dating among workers in the same organization. My experience suggests that generally it is unwise to be involved intimately with a working colleague. When work pressure is at its peak, you may be forced to choose in some way between your partner and your job.

I was exposed to this problem when a fine employee who worked in one area of an organization I served showed a marked decline in performance after she learned that the person with whom she was intimate was unhappily reassigned. In fact both performances went down. Colleagues are institutional co-workers and have a special professional working relationship that is very often jeopardized by intimacy.

Symbols of Success

A woman friend of mine is an insurance executive, and she told me recently that when she hung up her hard-earned degrees, awards, and honors in her office, as many of her male colleagues had done, this was perceived and labeled as self-serving. Men do not want women to come in as women, but yet when they play by men's rules, objectifying, posturing, and displaying symbols, they are also resented.

Myths

Men tend to make assumptions about women in the workplace, the same kind of sex-based myths they have learned in their personal lives. For example, in our company lunch room we have a poster,

---

**Your mother doesn't work here,
so please clean up your own mess.**

That is a learned, male response, picked up from what we have seen and done in the home; men make messes and women clean them up!

Similarly, the other day I called a law office to seek advice on an employee stock option plan. A woman answered, and I said, "May I please speak to an attorney?" She very indignantly replied, "I am an attorney. What do you want?" Of course she was right to feel slighted. I accepted the myth that a female answering the phone wouldn't be an attorney. Not sensitive on my part.

Handling Salary Differences

Do men relate as well with females who make more money than they do? Generally no. Why? It imposes the necessity of experiencing the woman in a totally new way. To fully cope with a woman making more money, the man must concede to her a value that his previous objectification of her says is impossible. It requires a radical and painful readjustment of his sense of reality and his place in that reality.

Does a woman care who makes the most money? Or for that matter does a woman in relationship care about any other kind of status? Not really. The relationship between them counts, not the salary, position, or title.

When two people have a healthy relationship, salary should not be a problem because the major value is their empathy and communication. That empathy is greatest when they accord one another equality. Then neither of them has a position to defend, they only have to nurture and defend the relationship.

Authority Figures

Men have had to learn to accept women as authority figures. Many are still uncomfortable with this. Probably some feel threatened by women. But it seems to me that what mainly disturbs men when dealing with women in authority is the fact that *these women often behave like men*. One of my first experiences as a young Marine Corps officer was to work with a senior woman major. I must tell you she remained feminine, *was a good leader*, and I responded. It is not necessary for women to act like men in order to exercise authority.

The Price for the Top

I must inject here again that to ask women to become like men greatly affects their personal relationships as well. A 1982 Korn/Ferry International study of 300 executive women documents the high number of women executives who are unmarried and/or childless. By contrast the majority of executive men are both married and have children. *It is not fair that women should have to pay such a price for executive status unless it is really their choice.*

Conditioning

One Saturday morning I suggested to a group of my senior sales representatives that we hold a breakfast meeting at my nearby home. I said, "I can't cook." One married senior male sales representative responded, "It's OK, we have Carol, Julie, and Donna." He wasn't being mean, only reflecting his conditioning. We must think of women as *talent*.

BEFORE I GO ON . . .

The Hite Report, *Women and Love*, which came out in late 1987, was written by a woman reporting on 4,500 women and their high level of dissatisfaction with what they call "love," which means their high level of dissatisfaction *with men*. I am quoting a few of Shere Hite's findings because I find them very appropriate to all I've suggested in this book.

The most frequently expressed reply (77 percent) is "He doesn't listen."

83 percent of women say they initiate most deep talks—and try very hard to draw men out:

Women: the Ones Who Try to "Make It Work"

98 percent of the women in this study say they would like more verbal closeness with the men they love; they want the men in their lives to talk more about their own personal thoughts, feelings, plans, and questions, and to ask them about theirs.

And one woman says what almost all women say: how much easier it is to talk to other women.

Most women want sex with feelings and love, most of the time.

The majority of women having affairs say they feel alienated, emotionally closed out, or harassed in their marriages.

What Are the Values of "Women's" Culture?
Its values include working together with others (rather than emphasizing competition), valuing friendship, listening with empathy, not being judgmental, trying to bring out the best in others, nurture, not dominate.

FINALLY—

The examples of the objectifying male vs. relational female behavior in the everyday world seem endless. I would guess by now you have thought of a few of your own. Let me now take the general concept—*Women tend to be more relational than men*—and move on to the direct implications for the workplace.

Part IV

Facts of Life

Now with respect to the workplace, this major difference between the sexes needs to be understood in terms of some major operational principles. When I examine the functioning of our culture, there appear to be different spheres of control or influence. The bottom line is this:

1. Women control sex. Most decisions about sexual intimacy will be made by women. Men can intimidate and do all kinds of things, but in fact, women are generally in control here. Now I don't mean simply the act of sex. I mean the whole emotional/physical arena of intimate relationships. Most intimate contact is finally decided upon by the woman. I will admit it is possible that a male may not want intimacy, and say no. But I won't bet my last dollar on these relatively rare instances.

2. Women control reproduction. Women have the awesome and wonderful ability to release life. I know that the male provides fifty percent of the child's genetic endowment; but it is the woman who carries it, nurtures it, and brings it into the world. This ability to give life has always carried with it a great deal of power and usually respect. However, this power does not transfer to the workplace in any way, except perhaps as a liability.

3. Women control most relationships. The main reason this is so is simple. They are the ones who primarily *care* about relationships! Obviously I am stretching a point here, but essentially this is true. They inevitably exert the major control over relationship because they *work* at it.

Thus women are enormously influential in regard to what many consider to be the most fundamental and the most important element in life, the *family* or *human survival unit*. When one considers that most acculturation takes place therein, and that the values and world view of the young are largely developed there, the family must be seen as having incalculable significance. This is particularly true because the nuclear family remains the place where most people experience intimate sharing and are given a sense of personal worth irrespective of their professional or functional activities. Women understand this best.

BUT THE KICKER IS . . .

4. Men control the workplace.

Men control the major institutions in our society. All institutions! Even if there's a women's bank, men control banking. Men control the military, men control the churches, the universities (despite the number of female faculty employed), medicine, politics, etc.

THEREFORE . . .

In my view these "facts of life" bear some very definite and frightening implications for the workplace. Women up to this point have only entered into the workplace in one of three ways:

1. They use their femininity. I mean femininity in the widest sense (the larger use of sexuality: flirtation or, more likely, subtle feminine manipulation of men), not necessarily explicit sexuality.

2. They are supportive or submissive. Or even worse they can be deferential, subordinate, and careful not to offend. **Or** . . .

3. They compete with men.

All three of these approaches are deficient, some of them more obviously than others. Most people find abhorrent the idea that women use their femininity to make their way in the workplace. Anyone who has to use her femininity in the office is degrading herself. Is it being done? Certainly! Do men encourage and respond to this type of behavior? Absolutely! Why? Because women know it is one way to get into and advance in the workplace. Is it the best way? Absolutely not!

Men say to me, "Where do they learn these behaviors?"

We taught them!

"I don't like women who use their sexuality to gain an advantage." My response is,

We encouraged them.

Women can also come into the workplace and be supportive, something they do well. When I hear this, even as a man, I know it is limiting. Nobody really wants a submissive female, whose main function is to be supportive of a man. That is a perversion of the inclination toward relationship; it's very boring, and even worse, you don't get much initiative and talent out of mere support or submission. This is a pattern that has also been encouraged in the workplace.

The only other way that women can break into the workplace is to compete on men's terms. And this is the most common approach, as I see it practiced. It has some holes as well. What does competition currently mean in the workplace? If you think about what I have been saying and look at the model, partly what it means for women to compete is that they must conform and objectify themselves.

Women learn how to compete, which means not only objectifying themselves but also objectifying others. They learn how to be tougher, how to be more aloof, how to be less emotional, how to be less relational. This attempt by women to duplicate male behavior carries with it some heavy and ironic penalties. Often the woman finds herself in a double bind in which she has relinquished some of her valuable relational qualities and is still chastized for her adaptation. She runs the risk of other women not liking her and the men not liking her either, as the illustrations below attempt to make clear.

The family picture is on HIS desk.
"A solid, responsible family man."

The family picture is on HER desk.
"Hmmm, her family will come before her career"

HE'S having lunch with the boss.
"He's on his way up."

SHE'S having lunch with the boss.
"They must be having an affair."

HE'S getting married.
"He'll get more settled."

SHE'S getting married.
"She'll get pregnant and leave."

Paths to Power
by Natasha Josefowitz

A businessman is aggressive.
A businesswoman is pushy.

He is careful about details.
She is picky.

He isn't afraid to say what he thinks.
She is opinionated.

He is a stern taskmaster.
She is difficult to work for.

"The Way We Are," *Good Housekeeping*
by Lois Wyse

I find that working women who are married face the additional challenge of having to play two roles each day, i.e., they have to objectify when at work, then when they go home to their spouse and children they have to be relational. A senior woman who works with me, when attending a social event with other employees, had to make these kinds of adjustments when involved in a three-way conversation between her husband and her boss. With the boss she strives to display objective behavior— they "get down to brass tacks" and talk "hard facts," with the husband she strives for relational behavior—she touches his arm and searches his eyes for subtle signs of approval or discomfort. She has to make all the adjustments! The men do not have to adjust. The male boss plays basically the same role at home and at work.

All three of these approaches to enter into the workplace—use of femininity, support/submission, and competition—deny the full capabilities of women, place strain on them, and hamper professional relationships based upon merit.

In my view:

The best and most appropriate way for women to achieve in the workplace is to be judged on competency alone.

But so far we men, but also to a limited extent women, have not made this easy. We deal with each other in the workplace from a perspective that we picked up as children and in the social world of dating. This makes it almost impossible for a woman to enter the male-dominated institutional world with as equal a chance for success as a man.

Without any deviation from the theme of this book, let me at least suggest that others, specifically other minorities, face much the same problem: a workplace that is beset with cultural bias, resulting in prejudice. When this is removed, competence and merit will prevail. I really believe this is possible, hence this book. I remember a talk I gave at a women's conference when a minority male executive said to me during the discussion period, "As a man I agree with what you are saying. But as a minority, I feel like a woman who has to make all the adjustments."

Part V

What We Can Do —
Achieving the Middle Ground

What can we do to facilitate men and women working together more effectively? How can we ensure a work environment that is free of preconceived attitudes toward sex roles and one that allows women to utilize their abilities and express the levels of competence that are appropriate for anyone's success? In my view a sound basis for harmonious relationships between the sexes in the workplace is contingent upon what I call *achieving the middle ground*.

So much emphasis in the literature and in training has been placed on women adapting to a traditional masculine behavior in order to be successful. I believe we must spend more time on the "middle ground" that encompasses the best of male and female characteristics. Margaret Sanger's book, *Women in the New Race*, sums up this point most effectively:

Her mission is not to emphasize the masculine spirit, but to express the feminine. Hers is not to preserve the man-made world, but to create a human world by the infusion of the feminine element into all its activities.

Both sexes need to look at sex roles in the workplace as a separate issue from private and personal behaviors. We must come to a new understanding of women in the workplace. But we must not fall under the illusion that men and women necessarily bring exactly the same strengths and potentials to the workplace. Additionally we must avoid those who are angry and who hope to bring extreme chauvinist or feminist views to our consciousness. Hopefully he or she isn't your boss!!!

We must move to a *middle ground* between our differing perspectives, from which we can accept and accommodate our differences and go on to use all of our working talent. As a businessman I can tell you,

We need all the talent we can get.

Acceptance and accommodation sound easy, but they will require great and consistent effort, especially from men. I am confident that this is possible, for men do not hesitate to make similar accommodations in other realms of their lives when they think the rewards are great enough. Perhaps as good an example as any comes from the world of sports. If you want to utilize the considerable talents of a quarterback like John Elway of the Denver

Broncos, the team makes adjustments to him, his talent, his strengths. He's your quarterback and you go with him.

Don Shula, it seems to me, came to the same conclusion at Miami, where he fashioned a radically different offense around the talents of Dan Marino. All great coaches and leaders take advantage of the players they have at the moment. They create something effective using what they have. What we have in the workworld today is a labor force composed of both women and men. Whether we like it or not, corporate football is now coed! We have women and we need women, so we must learn to adjust in order to take fullest advantage of their talents. We must go with our players!

I find the analogy of football particularly appropriate for several reasons. It is a sport that seems to embody many deeply held, male American values. Like the business world, football is highly competitive and goal-oriented. But equally important, football requires the blending of two significantly different perspectives. It demands the ability to be very objective about strategies and players. Simultaneously, it is a team effort and requires great relational skills in order to keep the team functioning as a harmonious and highly motivated unit. If you examine the most successful football teams of the last twenty years, I think you will find that they all exemplify this capacity to blend objectifying strategies with highly developed relational skills. This is exactly what men and women bring to the workplace!

Obviously this is not a book on football strategy, but I want to make clear what moving to the *middle ground of acceptance* means and to emphasize that we *can* do this if we fully understand and have a high enough level of commitment. In order to play winning, coed, corporate ball we're going to have to make adjustments. Maybe we'll have to have separate dressing rooms, maybe we will have to spend more time talking and listening, probably we will have to discipline some of our appetites, whatever. If we can make adjustments on the gridiron for new talent, we can certainly make adjustments in the corporate and institutional worlds to accommodate our most underutilized talent—women.

TO MEN I SAY:

It is time for *us* to accept and adjust

1. Be Men Of Courage. *You* deal with the

sexual issue. Don't make women fend for themselves.
Have courage and make clear, unequivocal statements
about sexual behavior in your workplace. I beg you, don't
leave it wide open and undefined. If you are a man who
can influence change, you need to make your position
clear immediately and conform to that position. Watch
for men who show patterns of sexual harassment, however
slight, and "head 'em off at the pass." This is every man's
responsibility. For example, behind my brother's desk he
has a large, painted photograph of his wife and children,
specially lighted. There is no question about his priorities.
Find a way, if you are in a managerial position, to say,
"We will perform our duties in a professional manner and
in a way that does not compromise or take advantage of
any woman. We will not use sex in executing any professional duties. Sexuality has no place in the work environment." Such clear sexual statements will immediately
elicit feelings of relief and respect from the women with
whom you work. You must talk about a professional
atmosphere and define it for all. If women hear and believe
you, they will feel safe and secure, able to focus on
business and show their talent.

When you make these clear sexual statements and ex-
hibit the integrity to maintain these statements, you will

find the quantity and quality of the work you receive from female co-workers will be equal to that of males. Why? Such statements say:

A. I value you as a human being and not as a sex object.

B. I'm not going to leave our professional relationship open and uncertain so that you are never quite sure what is really being asked of you.

I am also asking you to focus your male colleagues on the truth about sexual harassment, not the fiction. Men see sex where there isn't any; they often mistake *friendly* for *more*. Kathryn Stechert in *On Your Own Terms* asserts:

> Women are closely linked with sexuality in the minds of men. They are so accustomed to seeing women as sexual beings—not just lovers and wives, but also mothers, whose sex is critical to identity— that they see sex everywhere in their dealings with women.

For us to be aware of women as sexual creatures is inevitable and I think natural. But men, if you are capable of objectifying a person, as I maintain, then you also have the skill to "turn off" any feeling you wish in the same manner. You must do so in order to free the workplace of sexual overtones.

Look for women at someone else's workplace.

72

2. Develop A Professional Relationship.

You have no choice but to develop a *relationship* when you work with a woman. Now I know people are going to say "No, this is not right. That's not the way to operate in the workplace. What you are saying is sexist," etc. All these objections ignore the reality that women are inherently more relational than men. To work effectively with women, men must develop a *professional relationship* with them. This does not mean a brotherly, fatherly, protective, or personal relationship. These are inappropriate attempts to exercise family/socially learned patterns of authority over women. But you will need to have a relationship. You should deal with her in a way that recognizes her as human and that respects her values of trust, empathy, nurturance, connectedness, *and talent*.

I was asked, "Are you implying that men can work together with little or no relationship?" Yes, I am. But, you won't work well with a woman without a relationship.

A *personal* relationship should be replaced by a *professional*, respectful, valuing, trusting, cooperating alliance, which, if you think about it, defines a *colleague*. Yes, I am saying, men, think of and join women as *working colleagues*. When a good personal relationship develops between a man and a woman, it can be so very satisfying. So it is that when they become colleagues in the accomplishment of organizational goals, it too can be very satisfying.

3. Value And Respond To The Relational Nature Of Women.

A. Accept their loyalty and hard work. You normally will not have to worry about how hard she will work or her loyalty; she is relational.

B. Be consistent in sustaining a relationship; it is essential. Consistent behavior is one of the main ingredients in any successful relationship. When a man agrees to a pattern, method, or style of interaction with a female colleague, it must be respected and adhered to or the professional relationship breaks down.

C. Encourage women to use their intuition in decision making when appropriate. It has often been good outside the workplace.

D. Listen carefully to them. Learn to hear what they are really saying. Women's relational orientation often gives them a more global and contextual view of situations. They may consider more facets than one normally expects. Do not automatically dismiss a generalized statement because you don't see how it fits. Ask questions, there is much to be gained.

E. Learn body language. Learn body *language*, not bodies, for women say much in this way that many men seldom notice.

F. Talk to them, express your feelings. Don't stew over unproclaimed emotions. *Say what you mean and mean what you say.* Women can accept you so much more easily if you share openly. This reminds me of my feeble attempts to speak Arabic and Cantonese as I arrived in Egypt and Hong Kong for the first time, many years ago. They smiled at my clumsiness with their language, but greatly respected the fact that I was trying to communicate *in their language*. So it is with women. At least try to improve the areas in which you might not be so proficient: expressing feelings and talking.

G. Define the form of communication before you do business. When a man or woman comes into my office I make sure I understand what they desire. I say to them, "What exactly is it that you want to accomplish? Do you want to blow off steam? Do you want me to put my perspective on this issue? Or do you want me to make a decision?" It has to be clear what it is you both want to accomplish or you risk miscommunication. This is particularly important when men and women interact at work.

H. Think in terms of context as well as content. Explain *why* you are asking something of them. Explain how it relates to your agreed upon objectives. Do not bark orders without explanation.

I. Let them be interactive with their peers, subordinates, and superiors, it is more relational. Men tend to focus on their authority (position) power more than their personal (relational) power. Women interact a lot. That's fine.

J. Women will express their feelings. That's good. Men often withhold emotion because they fear it will reveal weakness and/or incompetence, a false presumption and one that is not shared by most women. To dwell on a woman's tears could lead to an inaccurate and unfair assessment of her abilities.

I was asked to comment on Congresswoman Patricia Schroeder's display of tears as she announced that she did not intend to seek the Democratic nomination for president. Politics aside, I stated that I was impressed with her sincerity, the importance of the decision to her, and the openness that she showed toward her constituents. Make no mistake, she is a strong woman.

4. Women Are Equal In Ability, Brains, And Competence. *We Know It, Let's Show It.*
Women may choose a different method, style, "road" to accomplish an organizational goal because of their special talents. When you believe they are competent regardless of their style, you will enhance their sense of confidence. You will help them maintain the sense of security to which they are fully entitled. Your positive actions regarding their competence allow them to exercise their talents most spontaneously and fully and will inevitably add to achievement in the workplace. *Invest in them and they will, in return, invest in you.*

5. Provide And Teach Them Leadership
Leadership is more than management. It purports to reconcile the needs of people in organizations with the goals of that organization to the end that all talent is maximized. *Leadership is not sexist. Leadership identifies, frees, encourages, and guides human talent.* It does not control, restrict, or reduce talent.

What I am saying, men, is: ensure that women are given good leadership. Provide them mentors, male or female, so they can learn about leadership and become leaders. We need them in this role. *Gender does not unleash ability, leadership does.* Men and women, each in their own way, are insecure toward the other in the workplace. Leadership helps reduce and guard against these insecurities. Are these strong statements? I hope so, because I want you to consider them carefully.

Leaders genuinely value all constituencies they serve. If you can't value each person or group you serve, then you can't effectively lead them. Often such a lack of valuing leads to prejudice. Wouldn't it be better for all of us to be led by someone who believes this?

6. Don't Always Look At Women, Think About Them.
Spend more time thinking about a concept or strategy such as I am suggesting here that will reduce sex bias and integrate women more fully into your work environment. If you don't accept my model, seek out those who can help you frame one or develop your own. But, please, don't ignore this important issue of sex roles in the workplace.

7. Be Sensitive To The Special Needs Of Working Women.
Despite much public pressure to have benefits that favor women extended to men, I must quickly suggest that for the moment we must seriously concentrate on essential benefits for women. Avoid using the "not fair to men" rhetoric until we at least have

women's salaries up to our level. *Women should not have to forego family and children to work; men don't.*

A. Find out what it is like. I recently asked a working woman, alone with two children, to describe her day.

> I get up at 4:30 a.m., fix breakfast, get the kids up, bathe and dress them, clean up a bit, think about dinner, drive one child to the babysitter, take the other one to school. At work I often receive a call about one of the children. By two-thirty I am always worried that my oldest gets transferred to his play-ground. In addition I must leave work exactly at five, otherwise I pay overtime to the child-care people. I pick them both up, drive home, fix dinner, help the eldest with homework, clean up the dinner dishes, get my clothes ready for work, and fall into bed.

B. Ask women what they need, and ask them for suggestions on how to achieve it.

C. Study programs that have worked in other institutions. I feel it would be inappropriate for me to comment extensively on particular types of programs. However, I wish to single out a few areas for your consideration that I have found important to the working women I value.

1. Meaningful maternity leave, without prejudice.
2. Day care availability, augmentation, and/or tax relief.
3. Flexible scheduling for family, especially child emergencies.
4. Insurance that covers well-baby care.

8. Remember, Salaries Are Still The Major Concern For Working Women. I have no problem standing tall for equal pay for equal work for men and women. I cannot say I am ready for the fight between nurses and police to decide who is worth more. If you want to help, please ensure or at least voice that all workers in your sphere of influence are entitled to equal pay for equal work.

Move women into areas and levels that are now mostly male. My sales force is now coed with equal pay and benefits. Let me tell you, it pays off. In any given month a man or a woman can top our sales-quota board. It's just talent showing.

A final comment on pay. Salaries support families, buy homes, bring societal respect, help when applying for bank loans, allow for safer living environments, and permit more opportunity for advancement consideration. *Women deserve these things too.*

9. Watch Your Language. I'm not referring to foul language, even though I find no place for it in the workplace. I mean, think about what you say to or in front of women. Endearments such as "honey," "sweetie" and "dear" top the list as offensive in my judgment. Phrases or statements that are simply out of line are next. I heard a major community leader introduce the first women members to a traditionally all-male civic club, and he ended with, "Now they can give up their noon Tupperware parties and attend the _____ club."

We are all guilty of this sometimes, and not only toward women. I recall describing my assistant dean on one of my Semester-at-Sea voyages to the press in Istanbul, Turkey, as a "sharp, bright, young Turk.'" Oops! Just be careful. You can do much damage with language.

I offer the following tips:

A. If it is gracious, respectful, and professional for men *and* women, it is OK to say it to either.

B. Treat men and women respectfully and on an equal basis in nonverbal areas as well, i.e., holding doors open, saying thank you, helping to carry items, etc.

C. Don't use poor humor to cover your insecurity around women. Think, and then say it naturally. "Would you like to have coffee with me to discuss the Smith deal?" Not, as I once heard, "Can your husband handle your having coffee with a sexy guy like me, business of course?"

10. Let Her Present Her Own Case In Evaluations.
Men do not always see what a woman does as valuable. Let her tell you. I learned this lesson well when a faculty member who happened to be female received an evaluation from me and after thinking about it, she came back and said, "I want to give you more data." I responded in my head with "Oh, no," but I listened. She continued, "You made no mention of one criterion you said was important in the beginning of the voyage, traveling with students in the country of call. I accept my evaluation, but here are the names of all the students I traveled with in each port and what we did.

And you are welcome to check with any of them." I did, and she had greatly enhanced the in-country experience of more than thirty- five students, more than most faculty, I dare to add. I raised her rating and learned my lesson well, to be sure to observe all of my own criteria *and* to let people present their own case, especially women, whom men often find difficult to evaluate.

Let me offer four simple steps that might be useful.

A. Since we often do not communicate well anyway, make abundantly clear to women what is expected, especially in terms of end-result performances.

B. Don't judge or hover over the paths used by women to reach the objectives agreed upon. Be available for counsel, offer guidance, and encourage them.

C. Be sure to value, evaluate, and judge on the accomplishment of the objectives, *nothing else*.

D. In addition to the forms and methods you use in evaluation, you might consider more latitude. Let her bring in letters, statistics, slides, fellow-workers' evaluations, anything that will ensure her a fair evaluation. I know this will sound unreasonable and time consuming to some, but it's good leadership and women need it, for our evaluation processes and forms are often not free of sex bias.

11. Encourage Women To Be And To Become. Educators have long known that students tend to rise to the level of expectation set for them by their teachers. The same is true for people, of either sex, in the workplace. Be sure that you are not unconsciously giving signals to women that your expectations for them are low, that you really do not believe that they can perform at a level equal to that of men. Help them take risks at work to show their best. Studies show that it is less likely for women to take risks at work. When you have a new or tough assignment, have a woman do it. She can do the job. If you don't believe this, then our talent-sensitive, creativity-centered, success-oriented system is going to be short of talent in the twenty-first century.

Remember, women, like men, need to be singled out for being "the best" at one thing and at the same time to feel and be a part of a team in any work environment.

12. Get It On The Table. Don't hide from this important issue, sex roles in the workplace. Acknowledge it. Take the lead and introduce training and experiences that bring this issue to the forefront. Do it with men and women *together*. As a major speaker for the Women in Business Conference in Colorado I was saddened to see so few men. It reminds me of the many international conferences I've attended where all the participants are from international agencies that favor international cooperation: believers talking to believers. It is not bad, but it would be so much better if interested people from other walks of life were encouraged to participate. They need to know and value this view in order to contribute positively in the future.

There are men and women available, inside and outside your organization, who are good at and committed to helping women and men get a healthy handle on this issue. *Find Them And Use Them.*

Given the few suggestions for modified behavior on the part of males outlined in this section, it is obvious the challenge to men is tremendous. It is a challenge that I feel men can and will meet because the stakes are high as we search for more talent.

TO WOMEN I SUGGEST:

1. Look At Our Motives, Not Our Mistakes.
Men will not always be playing by the same rules, in the same court, or with full understanding of female feelings, perspectives, or orientations. Hence, I suggest you try and determine our motives toward you, rather than dwell on our behavior or methods.

I once considered running for the U.S. Congress from Colorado, but during my very limited political involvement, I discovered that my remarks were invariably distorted and misunderstood. No one really tried to determine my motives for each position I took.

Please, as you come in contact with male behavior that seems inappropriate, try and see through to the motive. Thoughtless, destructive, or insensitive as the behavior might appear, try to respond according to the motive as you can best determine it. This I feel is *middle ground*.

I was talking with a small group at a university gathering some time ago and I was explaining what life on board ship with students is like. I said unthinkingly, "The *girls* outnumber the *men* two to one." That did it, one woman "jumped my case" with a verbal barrage that chilled the room. Was I wrong? Probably. But I said to her, "My motive was not to offend and by jumping on me so hard, you make me want to rebel against you and then it is hard for me to hear your message. However, I sincerely apologize for not being more sensitive." *Again, try and see our motive before you decide your reaction to our behavior.*

2. Don't Be Angry. Surely this is one of my most challenging prescriptions. Forget your bad experiences with men. Just as a tornado is a reality in Oklahoma, objectifying behavior from men is also a reality. Most men are not evil. And if we are to work together, it is essential for women to recognize our tendency to objectify people. Anger makes it impossible to communicate. And men are weak in this area already. Don't let your anger, even if derived from experience, make us less willing to communicate with you.

When Sex Bias Is Present Do Not React With Anger, But Do React.

React thoughtfully and honestly, focusing on how to communicate your feelings so we can grow and understand. Do not dwell on how to punish us.

3. Help Men Value You. I will admit that many men have not yet learned to value the relational skills that women possess. You can argue that men should appreciate these traits, but the fact of the matter is that we do not always see your special value. To accomplish this, to lead men to value you, I ask that you consider these few thoughts:

    A. Be as tolerant as possible of behavior that offends.

    B. Focus on your job competencies, not approval.

    C. Don't get sidetracked. Keep your focus on the important aspects of your work, your specific job objectives, and the general goals of your organization. Pettiness creeps in easily.

D. Use appropriate humor with us. We relax with humor. We posture and puff up less.

E. Ask for new and additional assignments and challenges. Be as involved as you can in the business at hand.

F. Be consistent toward us, even if our behavior changes toward you sometimes. We can learn about consistency from you.

G. Don't complain or hang around complainers. Men respond very poorly to complaining.

H. Study the belief system or corporate culture of your workplace and make sure you are comfortable with it. This is fundamental to work adjustment for anyone, but women are generally not advised in this area. They frequently select positions on the basis of the relationships they feel and expect from those with whom they are going to work. This is not enough.

I. Stretch yourself toward excellence always.

J. Value yourself and show it, or surely we won't be able to value you.

K. Train and learn with us on the issue of sex roles. Too many seminars are for women, by women. Reach out to us and include us in your seminars, discussions, and training. We need to learn how you feel.

4. Don't Listen To Those Who Would Have You Become Like Men.

You were born female, don't abandon your strengths. The workplace needs these strengths, especially today as we find more employee disaffection.

Paula Bern, author of *How To Work For A Woman Boss Even If You'd Rather Not*, suggests that "If a woman adopts everything we have termed masculine, the better off she will be." And Sandra Kurtzig, chairperson of ASK Computer Systems, Inc., in an article in *Electronic Engineering Times* states, "The best way for a woman to succeed in business is to have men forget she's a woman."

I respectfully ask that you *give men a chance to accept and include the feminine way in the workplace*. To do what Ms. Bern, Ms. Kurtzig, and others suggest only exacerbates the problem and precludes the special relational value of women and all that is feminine from becoming part of the workplace.

5. You, Too, Set Sex Role Boundaries.

Don't count on our courage totally to keep sexuality out of work. I have already conceded that men often force you to use feminine guile to get ahead, but this is destructive to both women and men. I implore you to play it straight, no sexual overtones, please. We are weak. We can't forget you are women, but we can handle it professionally if given a chance. *Sexuality is not appropriate power in the workplace for women or men.*

6. Business Is Business.

Having made all my previous points about the virtues that women bring to the workplace, there still remains a fundamental reality that we all have to face. Business is business. We must get the job done. That is why we're in business. I do not know how to make this reality easier, except to set down a few statements that define this place called work.

A. Perfection is not the standard, accomplished goals are. Often finishing all organizational assignments at an acceptable level is better than finishing only some at a perfection level.

B. Authority is given, not always earned, and leadership is hard to find.

C. Conflict is a part of work and heat goes with the territory.

D. Rules, regulations, and policies govern and control.

E. Objectifying something to deal with it is not bad, only a method. Women can use this characteristic male method without giving up their femininity, just as men can learn about relationship without giving up their masculinity.

F. Work is impersonal. You should have colleagues, not friends, at work because tough decisions may force you to choose between your work and your friends.

G. Organizations are slow to change, even if change is needed. They are like ships, slow to turn.

H. Creativity must remain within the bounds of the organizational goals.

I. All organizations are economic and have a bottom line.

J. Work involves risk taking and often decisions have to be made from the best of two poor choices.

K. Morality and ethics in business are different from personal morality because they include so many more people who believe differently and therefore can't be as fixed or rigid. Important, yes, but less perfect than those principles individuals can apply to their personal lives.

L. Power is hard to see sometimes. It is really *influence*. Women understand influence, therefore they understand *power*.

M. Negotiation and compromise are ongoing and essential to work.

N. Competition and pressure are a way of life at work.

O. Enjoy yourself. Yes, business is business, but the work experience should also be fulfilling.

IN SUMMARY . . .

What does all this mean to women? In short, organizational functioning, which has traditionally been defined by men, is often foreign to you. Come to work with realistic expectations, not idealized views of work or men. It is a place that *should* have basic honesty and integrity, well-defined objectives and goals, suggested and defined methods of operations to meet the goals, and protections from personal abuses and inappropriate uses of people.

I simply suggest you look for positions in firms that are willing to strike this deal.

You are given:

1. Opportunity, financial and personal;
2. A pleasant environment, in terms of benefits, work space, and personal treatment;
3. Leadership at all levels.

You are asked for:

1. Your best effort;
2. Your full attention to work goals;
3. An appreciative spirit, that is an appreciation for the workplace you select, its leaders, its goals and beliefs, even if they are sometimes imperfect.

7. Avoid Becoming A Barrier To Other Women.

This is a lose/lose posture. Women helping women is a win/win posture. It reminds me of some of my fellow doctoral students who, after receiving their degree, immediately espoused tougher standards for doctoral programs. They wanted to keep a closed shop, after they got theirs. *Be careful not to close the doors after you.*

Keep the doors open for those who want and need to follow you. All women will benefit if more make it to the top. Tara Roth Madden does a great job in her book, *Women versus Women,* where she writes of an "uncivil business war," describing conflicts between women of different age groups and different socio-economic classes. Please, ladies, don't go to war among yourselves.

8. Be A Team Player. For me this is the toughest to suggest and reduce to words. I don't mean to imply women can't and won't cooperate. Most do. I will stick my neck out, however, and suggest that with relationship and trust so important to most women it is possible for a "woman scorned" not to toss the ball to that person, even if it means winning the game.

Work is getting the job done. And often it means working with those who are not as kind, fair, or trustworthy as you might like or demand in your personal life. Be a team player anyway. This is not dishonest, this is *middle ground*.

9. Don't Leave Us Alone. Remember, you *civilize* us at home, in the world, *and* at work. A woman friend of mine was recently relating a comment she heard a man make, "There would be no reason for me to get up in the morning if it weren't for women." Yes, this could be construed as chauvinistic, but I choose to believe this is really a deep and abiding realization that men do recognize the need for feminine strengths in the world.

10. Remember, Personal Power Is Relational. Work power is given by the organization in title, authority, etc. A person needs both kinds of power to be really successful at work. *You* already have personal power through your relationship skills. You are halfway there before you start, except no one has told you this. Personal power is awesome when combined with organization/position power.

OF BOTH WOMEN AND MEN, I ASK:

1. Keep in mind, we are all insecure in some ways and the issue of sex role bias is clearly a form of insecurity felt by women and men alike. Be gentle toward each other as we try to eliminate sex bias in our workplaces.

2. The workplace should constitute only one-third of your life. Please accept the responsibility for the other two-thirds of your life. The other two-thirds are:

A. Personal development: Inner peace, self-respect, self-love, which should lead to a sense of personal worth *with* or *without* work.

B. Developed relationships: Committed, trusted, tested personal love relationships outside of work that constitute your human survival units.

The quality of these other two-thirds of your life directly affect the quality of your work life.

3. Differences between men and women are not good or bad, but essential, appropriate, and complementary. Neither men nor women gain by converting the other.

4. Even as I attempt to illustrate a fundamental difference between men and women, I realize, as you do, that we each have feminine and masculine characteristics, just in different proportions. That is the central unifying beauty of the human species.

5. And finally I ask you to ponder these questions. If magically, a baby boy and a baby girl could be sustained on an isolated island until adulthood:

A. Who would cuddle whom?

B. Who would protect whom?

C. Who would feed the children?

D. Who would climb the highest tree for coconuts?

E. Who would kill the wild boar to eat?

F. Who would dig the holes to find fresh water?

G. Who would cry when frustrated?

H. Who would keep this human group working together?

I. Who would cut down trees to build a boat?

I can't answer the questions for you. Each of you is entitled to your own view. However, let us share our answers in good faith as the basis for *middle ground,* so that we might learn that we can work together even if our answers are different.

Conclusion

I've spent years developing this thought piece. And I have spoken these words to many audiences. I believe this book, with Ron's help, accurately describes one reality. I offer it to you, the reader, as a small way of helping men and women to improve the quality of their work lives. I have found as I've made adjustments in my attitudes toward women that my pride has not been wounded, my work objectives have become more achievable, and I've enjoyed the workplace more. I feel that I am a better leader and worker for it.

I've written this book for men *and* women although I acknowledge that the book may appear a bit pro-female. This seemed necessary to me in a work age where men are not required, asked, or encouraged to make adjustments for sex-role discrepancies to the extent that women are.

The ultimate question is, of course, are we making any progress? Yes, I think so. I've seen improvements, and I feel we do have reduced sex bias in the work environment today. These improvements have been due largely to pioneering and courageous men and women and the enlightened leaders of our institutions, all of whom have pressed for changes that include total equality for women. I want to live to see the day when we *all* want and value both feminine and masculine characteristics in the workplace.

Lloyd S. Lewan

Bibliography

Abbey, Antonia, "Sex Differences in Attributions for Friendly Behavior: Do Males Misperceive Females' Friendliness?" *Journal of Personality and Social Psychology* 42, no. 5 (1982):830-838.

Astrachan, Anthony, *How Men Feel: Their Response to Women's Demands for Equality and Power*, Garden City, New York: Anchor Press/Doubleday, 1986.

Bakos, Susan C., *This Wasn't Supposed To Happen*, New York: The Continuum Publishing Co., 1985.

Baruch, Grace, Rosalind Barnett, and Caryl Rivers, *Lifeprints: New Patterns of Love and Work for Today's Woman*, New York: McGraw-Hill, 1983.

Berg, Barbara J., *The Crisis of the Working Mother*, New York: Summit Books, 1986.

Bernardin, H. John, ed., *Women in the Work Force*, New York: Praeger, 1982.

Bernard, Jessie, *The Future of Marriage*, New Haven: Yale University Press, 1982.

Bianchi, Suzanne M. and Daphne Spain, "American Women: Three Decades of Change". (U.S. Department of Commerce, Bureau of the Census, Special Demographic Analysis, Aug. 1983.)

Blau, Francine D. and Marianne A. Ferber, *The Economics of Women, Men, and Work*, Englewood Cliffs: Prentice-Hall, 1986.

Blaxall, Martha and Barbara Reagan, eds., *Women and the Workplace*, Chicago: University of Chicago Press, 1976.

Borman, Kathryn M., Daisy Quarm and Sarah Gideonse, *Women in the Workplace: Effects on Families*, Norwood, N.J.: Ablex Pub., 1984.

Brownmiller, Susan, *Femininity*, New York: Simon and Schuster, 1984.

Cannie, Joan K. *The Woman's Guide to Management Success*, Englewood Cliffs, New Jersey: Prentice-Hall, 1979.

Chafe, William H. *Women and Equality*, New York: Oxford University Press, 1977.

Chodorow, Nancy, "Family Structure and Feminine Personality," in M.Z. Rosaldo and L. Lamphere, eds., *Woman, Culture and Society*, Stanford: Stanford University Press, 1974.

———, *The Reproduction of Mothering*. Berkeley: University of California Press, 1978.

Colegrave, Sukie, *The Spirit of the Valley: The Masculine and the Feminine in Human Consciousness*, Great Britain: Virago Press, distributed by Houghton Mifflin Co., Boston, 1979.

Cowan, Connell and Melvyn Kinder, *Smart Women Foolish Choices: Finding the Right Men, Avoiding the Wrong Ones*, Signet, 1986.

Deaux, Kay, "Sex Differences," in T. Blass, ed., *Personality Variables in Social Behavior*, Hillsdale, N.J.: Ettbaum, 1977.

Degler, Carl N., *At Odds: Women and the Family in America From the Revolution to the Present*, New York: Oxford University Press, 1981.

Dowd, Maureen, "Many Women in Poll Equate Values of Job and Family Life," *The New York Times*, Dec. 4, 1983, A1ff.

Dowling, Colette, *The Cinderella Complex*, New York: Pocket Books, 1982.

Epstein, Sue, "Why Do Women Live Longer Than Men?" *Science 83* (Oct. 1983): 30-31.

Farrell, Warren, *Why Men Are the Way They Are*, New York: McGraw-Hill, 1986.

Forisha, Barbara, and Barbara H. Goldman, *Outsiders on the Inside: Women and Organizations*, Englewood Cliffs, N.J.: Prentice-Hall, 1981.

Fox, Mary F. and Sharlene Hesse-Biber, *Women at Work*, Palo Alto: Mayfield, 1984.

Fraiberg, Selma, *Every Child's Birthright: In Defense of Mothering*, New York: Basic Books, 1977.

Friedl, Ernestine, *Women and Men: An Anthropological View*, New York: Holt, Rinehart and Winston, 1975.

Gardenswartz, Lee and Anita Rowe, *What It Takes*, New York: Dolphin Books/Doubleday, 1987.

Gilligan, Carol, *In A Different Voice: Psychological Theory and Women's Development*, Cambridge: Harvard University Press, 1984.

Gross, Amy, "Thinking Like a Woman," *Vogue*, May 1982, 268ff.

Hacker, Andrew, "Women vs. Men in the Work Force," *The New York Times Magazine*, Dec. 9, 1984, 124ff.

Harragan, Betty L., *Games Mother Never Taught You: Corporate Gamesmanship For Women*, New York: Warner Books, 1977.

Hite, Shere, *Women and Love*, New York: Alfred A. Knopf, 1987.

Horn, Patrice and Jack C. Horn, *Sex in the Office*, Reading, Mass.: Addison-Wesley Publishing Co., 1982.

"How Executives See Women in Management," *Business Week*, June 28, 1982, 10.

Howe, Louise K., *Pink Collar Workers*, New York: Putnam, 1977.

Hyatt, Carole, *Women and Work: Honest Answers to Real Questions*, New York: M. Evans, 1980.

Jacobs, Nehama and Sarah Hardesty, *Success and Betrayal: The Crisis of Women in Corporate America*, Franklin Watts, 1986.

Jardim, Anne and Margaret Hennig, *The Managerial Woman*, New York: Anchor Press/Doubleday, 1977.

Kahn-Hut, Rachel, Arlene K. Daniels and Richard Colvard, *Women and Work: Problems and Perspectives*, New York: Oxford University Press, 1982.

Kenniston, Kenneth and the Carnegie Council on Children, *All Our Children: The American Family Under Pressure*, New York, 1977.

Korn/Ferry International, "Profile of Women Senior Executives," 277 Park Avenue, New York, 1982.

Kreps, Juanita M., ed., *Women and the American Economy: A Look to the 1980's*, Englewood Cliffs: Prentice-Hall, 1976.

Kurtzig, Sandra, "Women As Corporate Executives," *Electronic Engineering Times*, Monday, October 27, 1986.

Lewenhak, Sheila, *Women and Work*, New York: St. Martin's, 1980.

Maccoby, Eleanor, and Carol Jacklin, *The Psychology of Sex Differences*, Stanford, Calif.: Stanford University Press, 1974.

MacKinnon, Catherine A. *Sexual Harassment of Working Women*, New Haven: Yale University Press, 1979.

Madden, Tara R., *Women vs. Women: The Uncivil Business War*, New York: Amacom, 1987.

Malia, Jinx, *Breaking Into the Boardroom*, New York: G.P. Putnam's Sons, 1986.

Malloy, John T., *Dress for Success*, New York: Peter H. Wyden Publishing Co. 1975.

McBroom, Patricia, *The Third Sex; The New Professional Woman*, New York: William Morrow & Co., 1986.

Mead, Margaret, *Sex and Temperament*, New York: William Morrow and Co., 1963.

———, *Male and Female*, New York: William Morrow and Co., 1967.

———, "A Proposal: We Need Taboos on Sex at Work," *Redbook*, April, 1978.

Nieva, Veronica and Barbara A. Gutek, *Women and Work: A Psychological Perspective*, New York: Praeger, 1981.

Norwood, Robin, *Women Who Love Too Much: When You Keep Wishing and Hoping He'll Change*, Los Angeles: J.P. Tarcher, 1985.

Pinkstaff, Marlene and Anna Wilkinson, *Women at Work: Overcoming the Obstacles*, Reading, Mass.: Addison-Wesley, 1979.

Rubin, Lillian B., *Intimate Strangers: Men And Women Together*, New York: Harper & Row, 1984.

Sanday, Peggy R., *Female Power and Male Dominance: On the Origins of Sexual Equality*, New York: Cambridge University Press, 1981.

Sanger, Margaret, *Women and the New Race*, Oxford, New York: Pergamon, 1969.

Smith, Ralph E., ed., *The Subtle Revolution: Women at Work*, Washington, D.C.: The Urban Institute, 1979.

Stechert, Kathryn, *On Your Own Terms: A Woman's Guide to Working with Men*, New York: Vintage/Random House, 1987.

Strathern, Marilyn, *Women in Between: Female Roles in a Male World*, New York: Seminar Press, 1972.

U.S. Department of Commerce, Bureau of the Census, *Historical Statistics of the United States, Colonial Times to 1970*, Bicentennial Edition, Part 1, 1975.

U.S. Department of Commerce, Bureau of the Census, Current Population Reports, Consumer Income Series P-60, no. 148, *Characteristics of Households and Persons Receiving Selected Noncash Benefits: 1983*, Table 1.

U.S. Department of Labor, *Employment and Training Report of the President, 1982*, Table A-1.

U.S. Department of Labor, Bureau of Labor Statistics, *Employment and Earnings 32*, no. 1 (January 1985).

_____, *Time of Change: 1983 Handbook on Women Workers*, U.S. Department of Labor, Bulletin 298.

Wallace, Phyllis A., ed., *Women in the Workplace*, Boston: Auburn House, 1982.

Williams, Marcille G., *The New Executive Woman*, New York: Mentor-NAL, 1977.

About the Authors

Lloyd S. Lewan is presently executive vice president and vice chairperson of the board of Lewan & Associates, Inc., one of the largest, locally owned office equipment dealerships in the nation. For eighteen years he served as executive dean and director of academic affairs for the Institute of Shipboard Education. The Institute and the University of Pittsburgh, together, operate the international studies program, Semester at Sea. This former U.S. Marine Corps officer, college teacher, and administrator holds a doctoral degree from Oklahoma State University. His many invitations to speak to a wide variety of audiences attest to his effectiveness and popularity as a major voice on workplace issues today. A few of the organizations at which he has recently spoken include: Federal Women's Programs for the Department of Defense, the University of Arkansas at Little Rock, the U.S. Geological Survey, the I.R.S., Ford Motor Company, and U.S. West.

Ronald G. Billingsley served for five years as a naval officer before earning his Ph.D. and becoming a college

English professor. For the past fifteen years he has worked as a writing consultant and taught courses in American literature and interdisciplinary studies at the University of Colorado. Dr. Billingsley's research and teaching interest in American culture prompted him to collaborate with Dr. Lewan in the writing of *Women in the Workplace: A Man's Perspective*.

For Information:

Information regarding speeches, seminars, training, audio or video tapes, and additional copies of this book may be obtained by writing to:

Dr. Lloyd S. Lewan
Remington Press
P.O. Box 24187
Denver, Colorado 80224-0187
(303) 320-8714

notes

notes

notes

notes